For the puffins of
Dancing Ledge

Copyright © 1984 by Deborah King.
Text Copyright © 1984 by Jonathan Cape Ltd.
First published in Great Britain in 1984 by
Jonathan Cape Ltd.

First U.S. Edition
1 2 3 4 5 6 7 8 9 10

**Library of Congress Cataloging in Publication
Data**

Lewis, Naomi
  Puffin

  Summary: Traces the life of a young sea bird born
on an island off the northern coast of Scotland.
  1. Puffins – Juvenile literature. [1. Puffins]
I. King, Deborah, 1950- ill. II. Title.
QL696.C42L48 1984 598'.33   83-23864

ISBN 0-688-03783-6
ISBN 0-688-03784-4 (lib. bdg.)

Printed in Italy by New Interlitho, SpA, Milan

PUFFIN
DEBORAH KING

Story told by Naomi Lewis

LOTHROP, LEE & SHEPARD BOOKS
NEW YORK

Puffin was born one Midsummer Day in an old rabbit burrow on an island off the northern coast of Scotland. Both parent birds had taken turns in guarding the egg for the five weeks before it hatched; now both worked hard to bring small fish to feed the little bird. In his dark nursery he was often alone, for puffins lay only one egg each season. But, outside, the air was filled with the noise of sea birds – guillemots, razorbills, gannets, kittiwakes, and other puffins like his own parents.

By THE end of July Puffin, now six weeks old, had grown into a fat, contented little fledgling. But this safe and sheltered time came to an end. The tired parent birds returned to the sea, to drift away and molt their feathers and change to winter coloring. Puffin waited in the nest a week or more, then ventured out – not in the strange, disturbing daylight, but at night. He saw the moonlit water and scrambled toward it through the rough grass (for he had not yet learned to fly), hopped over the edge of the cliff, dropped down two hundred feet, and spent his first night in the open splashing about in the shallows.

BY DAYLIGHT Puffin had been washed into deeper waters. He drifted with the tide, floating up and down in the swell. The light brought dangers too. Powerful gulls, soaring with the wind, began to swoop down from the sky in search of easy prey. To escape, Puffin dived beneath the waves.

At once he felt at home.

WITH HIS small but muscular wings and strong webbed feet for steering, Puffin soon became a skilled underwater swimmer. He quickly learned to fly and to dive for fish like the other birds around him: the guillemots and razorbills; the great cormorants, who skimmed the floor of the sea; the gannets, who pierced the waves like arrows. Puffin now had to teach himself how to live as an ocean bird. The guillemots and razorbills belonged, like himself, to the auk family. But they left the nest after only two or three weeks, and their parents stayed with them for several weeks to teach and protect them. Puffin had had seven sheltered weeks in which to grow, before taking to the open sea by himself.

DURING the next five months – Puffin's first winter – he journeyed away from land into the mid-Atlantic. Driven along by winds and tides, he traveled far. In storms, when the waves rose high, he would lightly bounce off the breakers and dive below. As he swam he remained alone, as he had been from the start.

IN FEBRUARY Puffin reached the coast of Newfoundland, over three thousand miles from his Scottish home. A vast stretch of glittering ice lay before him. The air was clear and still; the only sounds came from crackling ice and from the very young seal pups calling out for their mothers. For it was here that the harp seals came every year to breed.

Wherever the mother seals had broken the ice into pools, Puffin could dive into the sea for food and shelter.

When the spring came, and the frozen space began to melt, he was joined by hundreds of Canadian puffins. They had returned from ocean wanderings to the place where they were born, to begin their own breeding season.

PUFFIN spent the summer in Newfoundland; but when winter returned he became restless and took to the sea again. There he met the greatest danger he was ever likely to know, for the death it brought came slowly and horribly. While swimming underwater he saw a dark shape overhead, cutting out all the light. He raced along, afraid but not knowing why, until he came to a break in the murk above; then he rose to the surface. Around him lay a great stretch of thick dark slime, filled with struggling shapes of birds and other living creatures who would never be able to free themselves. The oil slick drifted on toward the shore – and Puffin flew on and on, as far away as he could.

BUT THERE were other dangers as Puffin traveled the northern seas the next year and the next. Among these were the giant skuas diving down from above in search of food, and the schools of sharks rising up from deep below. Worse still were the trawl nets, where Puffin saw cormorants and other birds helplessly trapped. But he had no fear of the humpbacked whales off the coast of Nova Scotia. He had drifted there with the Labrador current, and as he rested in a secluded bay he was gently rocked up and down by the spouting of these whales.

THREE YEARS passed. The summer was over and with the strong September winds behind him Puffin set out across the Atlantic for the Scottish island that was his own birthplace. He arrived at last in March, with hundreds of other puffins who also had made the long ocean journeys, spending many weeks at sea. Nervous about the land, they wheeled over the cliffs for several days, continually returning to the water.

Finally they touched down. And Puffin now was back where he began.

ALL OVER the island the cliff tops seemed alive with birds, hopping over boulders, inspecting burrows, and starting their spring courtship. Puffin too had found a mate, and like the other birds was bowing and dancing before her, shifting from one foot to another, rapping beaks with her, until at dusk they flew together down to the sea.

IN THE FIRST light of morning, the flocks of puffins rose from the sea and flew back to the cliffs to choose their nesting sites. Some set about cleaning old burrows, or homes from an earlier season. Some, who were not so lucky, hollowed out new ones, using their beaks for spades and their feet for shovels. When the holes were ready, old or new, the birds flew off to look for nesting materials. The air was full of birds returning with stalks and grasses in their beaks.

At the entrance to Puffin's burrow a rabbit appeared. It was part of his own home, after all. But at the sight of so many birds on his quiet island he turned and vanished down a back passage far into the cliff. Puffin never saw that rabbit again.

SOON THE female birds began to lay their single white eggs. But not every puffin had found or made a home, and often a male bird would battle with another over a wanted site. The two would lock bills together and tumble over the cliff, refusing to separate until they hit the water. Then they would fly back to the top and repeat this performance until one admitted defeat. Puffin himself was involved in such a fight. But he was no loser, and he kept his home.

FOR MORE than thirty days Puffin helped his mate to guard and tend the egg, and toward the end of June their chick was hatched. Now the little bird had to be fed constantly. By swimming zig-zag through shoals of sand eels or small fish, Puffin was able to bring back six or seven at a time, stacked head to tail across his beak. In strong winds, when landing was quite difficult for a smaller bird, the powerful gulls would try to steal the catch. But Puffin escaped each time, and his nestling did well.

PUFFIN and his mate fed their chick without rest for six weeks. By the end of July it was time for them to leave the fat little creature, as they themselves had once been left. Puffin and his mate returned to the water and floated away into the ocean, to renew their strength. For a week or more the fledgling stayed alone in the nest, growing thinner and knowing hunger for the first time. Then, one night, it ventured out of the burrow, made its way over the cliffs and into the waves, to discover the marvelous worlds of air and sea as puffins have always done.